WHAT'S THE POINT OF THIS BOOK?

I hope you enjoy working through this book. It took months of development and years of playing with ideas before that. **If you like it, please tell your friends and write a review on Amazon!** We are a family business: customer recommendations make an enormous difference.

This series grew out of my more exam-oriented resources in 11 Plus Lifeline. So many parents got in touch to ask for further writing materials, sometimes for exam preparation and sometimes just because their children enjoyed being creative, that I decided to to do something about it. I wanted the resources to be about more than exams, and I wanted them to be suitable for people all across the English-speaking world.

RSL Creative Writing focuses on descriptive writing and short stories, but the series also includes packs covering letters, emails and persuasive essays. There are even opportunities to continue a story by a famous author, blending your style with theirs.

The guiding idea behind this series is that a young person's creativity deserves respect. Far too often, children are taught to write childishly, with a focus on shortcuts: *use lots of adjectives, add these ten "wow words"*, and so on. However, I've found that many children can write as well as adults, if only they are shown how. By teaching them cheats rather than encouraging them to think about language in a mature way, grown-ups do them no favours.

Children should be shown the power of words. They should be taught that language is an enormous toolbox, full of possibilities but requiring careful judgment. The challenge we face is to choose words effectively, finding the best ways to shape our readers' thoughts and feelings.

Learning to write well involves learning to read well. Everybody finds it difficult to spot weaknesses in their own writing. For this reason, if we want to see things from a reader's point of view, it's best to start by looking at somebody else's work. That's why this book is full of examples. Mind you, not all of them are *good* examples!

Confident children will be able to use these resources independently. However, the series is likely to be even more useful when parents and children discuss things together … especially if both of you attempt the exercises and compare your answers. Try it! You may be surprised by the results.

Happy writing!

Robert

ALSO AVAILABLE

RSL Creative Writing: further volumes

11 Plus Lifeline (printable resources for all 11+ subjects):
www.11pluslifeline.com

RSL 11+ Comprehension: Volume 1

RSL 11+ Comprehension: Volume 2

RSL 11+ Comprehension, Multiple-Choice: Volume 1

RSL 11+ Comprehension, Multiple-Choice: Volume 2

RSL 11+ Maths

RSL 8+ to 10+ Comprehension

RSL 13+ Comprehension

GCSE Maths by RSL

GCSE Spanish by RSL

GCSE French by RSL

GCSE German by RSL

RSL Creative Writing: Book 3

by Robert Lomax

Published by RSL Educational Ltd

Copyright © RSL Educational Ltd 2021

Company 10793232

VAT 252515326

17 Woodside Road, Bricket Wood, St Albans

Registered in England & Wales

Design and typesetting by

Heather Macpherson at Raspberry Creative Type

Images © Shutterstock.com.

www.rsleducational.co.uk

CONTENTS

For advice on creative writing,
exam preparation and more,
visit www.rsleducational.co.uk/blog

PACK 7
Similes

HOW TO CONJURE UP SIMILES LIKE A LITERARY WIZARD

This pack will teach you to come up with similes that work brilliantly – and to avoid ones that don't!

SIMILES

This pack will teach you to come up
with similes that work brilliantly –
and to avoid ones that don't!

A simile is a type of figurative language that compares two things, almost
certainly using "**like**" or "**as … as**".

 A simile's job is to help the reader imagine what is going on
more vividly than they could without it.

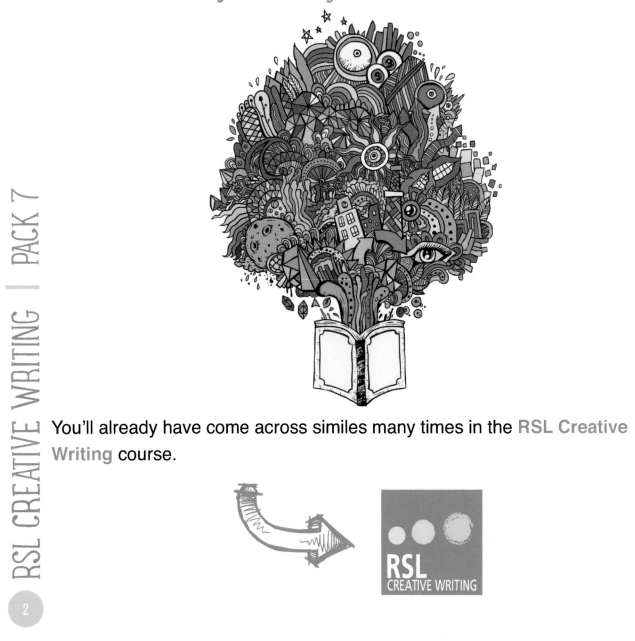

You'll already have come across similes many times in the RSL Creative
Writing course.

RSL
CREATIVE WRITING

EXERCISE 1: SPOT THE SIMILE

Which of the following sentences contain similes?

 I like to eat crisps.

 Karl slept as soundly as a well-fed baby.

 As often as possible, I watch new movies at the cinema.

 Just like that, it was over.

 You're not as perky as normal.

 They don't like each other.

 A good simile is like a fire in a biscuit tin.

 Tobias has the sort of face you don't easily remember.

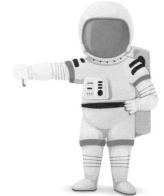

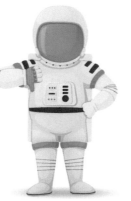

EXERCISE 1: ANSWERS

These are the only similes in the list:

 Karl slept as soundly as a well-fed baby.

 A good simile is like a fire in a biscuit tin.

Both of these compare one thing to another, and both are figurative: they are designed to create an impression, not to say something that is literally true.

I don't know quite how **"a good simile"** *can be* **"like a fire in a biscuit tin"**, *but it's definitely a simile!*

Most of the other sentences use **"like"** or **"as"** in misleading ways.

Several of them use **"like"** to show enjoyment or preference (**"I like"**), or in idiomatic phrases such as **"just like that"**, meaning **"suddenly"**.

 An idiom is a phrase with a meaning that can't easily be worked out from the words it contains. English idioms are often a piece of cake for native speakers, but language learners can be tied in knots by phrases like "once in a blue moon": they frequently get the wrong end of the stick.

"As possible" and **"as normal"** aren't figurative or poetic expressions.

 You might also notice that while a simile will normally compare something to another thing – involving a noun such as **"fire"** or **"baby"** – **"possible"** and **"normal"** are adjectives.

The last sentence, about Tobias's face, doesn't make any comparisons, so it certainly doesn't contain a simile!

There are four similes in the following paragraph. What do you think of them?

 Which similes are effective?

 Which similes don't work?

Ivor flailed like a scarecrow in a hurricane. He might not have learnt the steps, but the one thing he would not do in this dance showcase was stand in the middle of the stage like a dead fish, while everybody else pirouetted around him. He would keep dancing – keep moving – continue to fling his limbs around him with all the energy he could muster like a general lining up their troops, until, whether by sheer will power or brute luck, he settled into the beat. That moment would come, he had no doubt; and once he got hold of the rhythm, he would hang on as tightly as a panda with a stick of bamboo.

In my opinion, these similes are a mixed bag! ("**A mixed bag**" is a metaphor … but there will be more about those in a later pack.)

"**Ivor flailed** like a scarecrow in a hurricane" is, in my opinion, a very effective simile. It suggests the frantic desperation of his movements in an amusing way.

 More subtly, it also suggests that for all the chaos of his movements, there is a certain focus to them – just as a hurricane's winds will tend to send things in one direction. It might also imply that everything happens with him anchored to a single spot on the stage.

 It's worth bearing in mind that while a simile says that two things are *similar*, it doesn't claim that they are *alike*. Just because I compare Ivor to a scarecrow, it doesn't follow that he is stuffed with straw!

If a simile seems to work in the ways that matter most, you can expect a reader to use their common sense to judge where the similarities end.

Saying that Ivor doesn't want to stand on stage "like a dead fish" makes a certain amount of sense: a dead fish would look pretty out of place! But then we run into a problem, because a dead fish does not "**stand**" … for that matter, even a live fish would be unlikely to.

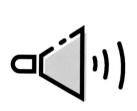 This is an example of the difficulties that you can get into if you pick a simile because it matches just one characteristic of the thing you are describing, but you don't think about the other ideas it might suggest.
The scarecrow image fitted the scene in several ways; the dead fish didn't!

 "Like a general lining up their troops" isn't the worst way of describing somebody storing up their energy to attack a problem, although it's hard to think of one person's energy being like lots of separate soldiers. But does it make sense when we are talking about somebody who is throwing their limbs around wildly?

The final simile, "as tightly as a panda with a stick of bamboo", might or might not help. If you think of pandas as fanatical bamboo-munchers, it will make sense to you; but if you imagine them as relaxed and snoozy, it won't fit. In the end, does this simile add anything that wouldn't have been clear from "**he would hang on tight**" (or "**tightly**")?

From these examples, we can come up with some simple rules for deciding whether a simile is good or bad.

 A simile is good if it makes a thing easier to imagine than it would otherwise be.

 A simile is good if it intensifies the reader's emotional response to your writing.

 A simile is bad if it doesn't help the reader to imagine things clearly or if it creates confusion.

 A simile is bad if it could suggest something different from what you want the reader to imagine.

 A simile is bad if it pulls focus from more important things in your writing.

EXERCISE 2: GOOD OR BAD?

Decide whether each of the following similes

 is probably a good choice

 is probably a bad choice

 might be good or bad, depending on the context

Write "**good**", "**bad**" or "**depends**" next to each one.

She had a voice like a coffee grinder. ....

The rocket hit the ground like a house. ....

The carpet was as smooth as puppy fur. ....

The smell was as pungent as laundry. ....

Donald wrote like a cheetah. ....

EXERCISE 2: MY ANSWERS

She had a voice like a coffee grinder. .... *Good* ....

➤ I can imagine exactly what this person's voice sounds like!
Remember that "**like**" doesn't mean "**exactly the same as**".

The rocket landed like a house. .... *Bad* ....

➤ How does a house "**land**"? In what situation would this happen?

The carpet was as smooth as puppy fur. .... *Good* ....

➤ I can clearly imagine the texture of this carpet.

The smell was as pungent as fresh laundry. .... *Depends* ....

➤ How pungent *is* fresh laundry? It depends what it's been washed in!
A different simile might be clearer.

However, this simile might come in a story where laundry has already been discussed. If we know that the laundry in this house smells strongly of lavender, the simile will make perfect sense.

Donald wrote like a cheetah. .... *Bad* ....

➤ "**Like a cheetah**" similes always make me smile – but they are rarely a good choice!

If you'd like some ideas about why, look at the creative writing tips on the RSL Educational blog (**rsleducational.co.uk/11-plus-creative-writing**), where I talk about cheetah similes in detail.

EXERCISE 3: FORMING SIMILES

The first step before coming up with a simile is to **imagine the scene very clearly**. Form a detailed picture in your mind, feeling the emotions that go with it.

Once you've done this, you can let your mind play with similar feelings and ideas from other situations, until you find a good match. Allow your mind to move freely: don't try to force your imagination.

Test each idea. Is it a good one?

Once you've found an idea that you like, experiment until you find the best form of words to convey it.

Don't try to think of a simile that you've read elsewhere. If you want an image that perfectly matches the ideas in your mind, you will need to come up with your own!

➡ Fill the gaps in the following sentences with your own original similes.

You'll have two chances to describe each thing: once with "**like**" and once with "**as ... as**". Look for two completely different approaches each time!

He brushed his teeth as .... as

....

He brushed his teeth like ....

....

The clouds scattered like ....

....

The clouds scattered as .... as

....

The explosion was as .... as

....

The explosion was like ....

....

Like ....

.... she lifted him by the collar.

As .... as ....

.... she lifted him by the collar.

EXERCISE 3: MY ANSWERS

 He brushed his teeth as rhythmically as a factory robot.

 He brushed his teeth like a jeweller polishing gemstones.

Both these images suggest people who care about cleaning their teeth, but in different ways.

The first person seems to be focused on doing a good, consistent job. They have an efficient system, and they follow it automatically.

The second person loves his teeth. He tries to make each one sparkle!

 The clouds scattered like a pod of whales, diving out of sight into the deep blue.

 The clouds scattered as nimbly as iron filings fleeing a magnet.

Both these images imply that the clouds clear rapidly. The main difference is that the first one makes them seem massive, while the second makes them light and trippy.

More subtly, the first image suggests that they might "**scatter**" in the same general direction, like a group of social animals, whereas the second implies that they retreat outwards from a shared central point.

Finally, the first image makes clear that the clouds disappear from view, "**out of sight**", whereas the second sees them spread out across the sky.

The explosion was as concussive as a mallet-blow to the head.

 The explosion was like the end of time.

The first image implies a physical sensation, whereas the second focuses on the overwhelming emotional effect of the blast.

 Like an enraged grizzly, she lifted him by the collar.

 As deftly as a child swiping a bag of sweets behind a shopkeeper's back, she lifted him by the collar.

It isn't usually a good idea to develop a simile at as much length as my second image. Here it's done for comic effect.

In all these cases, the different choices of simile suggest quite different things about the characters and settings being described.

For this reason, you have to choose similes with great care. It isn't enough to think "**I need a simile for tooth cleaning**" and use the first idea that comes to mind.

First, you have to work out exactly *how* your character is cleaning their teeth.

Then you need to find *just the right simile to match*.

EXERCISE 3: TIME FOR ANOTHER TRY!

Now that you've had a go and seen my examples, can you come up with some different similes to describe the same events?

He brushed his teeth as .... as

....

He brushed his teeth like ....

....

The clouds scattered like ....

....

The clouds scattered as .... as

....

The explosion was as .... as

....

The explosion was like ....

....

Like ....

.... she lifted him by the collar.

As .... as ....

.... she lifted him by the collar.

EXERCISE 4: NORMAN

Your choice of simile can completely change your meaning.

The following passage is missing a simile:

> Clarissa eased the storeroom door aside. "What are you doing in there, Norman?" she whispered. Norman froze, then slowly turned his head towards her.
>
> His smile was like . . . . "You're about to find out," he said.

What was Norman's smile like? The whole meaning of the passage hangs on this detail.

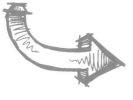 After reading each of the following versions, draw a simple sketch of Norman's smile, and write a sentence to say what's likely to happen next.

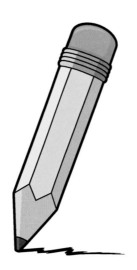

Here's an example:

Clarissa eased the storeroom door aside. "What are you doing in there, Norman?" she whispered.

Norman froze, then slowly turned his head towards her. His smile was like a blast of sunshine on a winter day. "You're about to find out," he said.

Norman's smile:

What's going to happen next?

Clarissa's friends break out in "Happy Birthday" behind her, while

Norman walks towards her with an enormous cake.

Version 1

Clarissa eased the storeroom door aside. "What are you doing in there, Norman?" she whispered. Norman froze, then slowly turned his head towards her.

His smile was like light flashing on a blade. "You're about to find out," he said.

Norman's smile:

What's going to happen next?

....

....

....

Version 2

Clarissa eased the storeroom door aside. "What are you doing in there, Norman?" she whispered. Norman froze, then slowly turned his head towards her.

His smile was like soothing balm. "You're about to find out," he said.

Norman's smile:

What's going to happen next?

....

....

....

Version 3

Clarissa eased the storeroom door aside. "What are you doing in there, Norman?" she whispered. Norman froze, then slowly turned his head towards her.

His smile was like taut wire. "You're about to find out," he said.

Norman's smile:

What's going to happen next?

....

....

....

EXERCISE 4: EXAMPLE ANSWERS
Version 1

Clarissa eased the storeroom door aside. "What are you doing in there, Norman?" she whispered. Norman froze, then slowly turned his head towards her.

His smile was like light flashing on a blade. "You're about to find out," he said.

Norman's smile:

What's going to happen next?

The door closes itself behind Clarissa and red-caped vampires step forward from the shadows.

"**Like light flashing on a blade**" suggests that Norman is gleefully expecting violence.

Version 2

Clarissa eased the storeroom door aside. "What are you doing in there, Norman?" she whispered. Norman froze, then slowly turned his head towards her.

His smile was like soothing balm. "You're about to find out," he said.

Norman's smile:

What's going to happen next?

He puts a finger to his lips and beckons to her. In a cage in the corner are four newborn rabbits, suckling their mother.

A smile "**like soothing balm**" suggests that Norman has something happy to share – something that makes him feel calm and contented.

Version 3

Clarissa eased the storeroom door aside. "What are you doing in there, Norman?" she whispered. Norman froze, then slowly turned his head towards her.

His smile was like taut wire. "You're about to find out," he said.

Norman's smile:

What's going to happen next?

Norman steps back to reveal a stolen painting. "It's time you knew the truth", he murmurs, fixing his eyes on hers.

"Like taut wire" implies a tight, contained smile. It suggests that Norman feels tense, but perhaps still hopes things will turn out well.

EXERCISE 5: MIRA

Here's another passage with a missing simile:

The curtain rose, and the audience gasped as one as they saw Mira standing in the spotlight . . . . With the clatter of a drum riff, the band came to life around her.

This time I'll give you a sketch and an indication of what's going to happen next. You need to come up with a simile that makes sense in the light of these things. You can choose a simile beginning with "**like**" or "**as**".

Version 1

Mira's posture:

What's going to happen next?
Mira drops the microphone and flees.

The curtain rose, and the audience gasped as one as they saw Mira standing in the spotlight . . . .

With the clatter of a drum riff, the band came to life around her.

Version 2

Mira's posture:

What's going to happen next?

Mira gives the best performance of her life.

The curtain rose, and the audience gasped as one as they saw Mira standing in the spotlight..
....
....

With the clatter of a drum riff, the band came to life around her.

Version 3

Mira's posture:

What's going to happen next?

Mira stops the band and starts shouting insults at the audience.

The curtain rose, and the audience gasped as one as they saw Mira standing in the spotlight..

....

....

With the clatter of a drum riff, the band came to life around her.

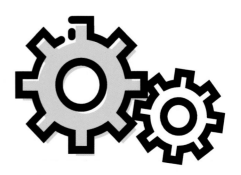

EXERCISE 5: EXAMPLE ANSWERS
Version 1

Mira's posture:

What's going to happen next?

Mira drops the microphone and flees.

The curtain rose, and the audience gasped as one as they saw Mira standing in the spotlight like a fugitive cornered at gunpoint. With the clatter of a drum riff, the band came to life around her.

From the picture we can see that Mira is terrified – and we know that she is about to drop her microphone and run away. When looking for a suitable simile, I need to help the reader imagine a situation so terrifying that their first instinct would be to flee.

The simile that I've chosen implicitly compares the audience to a squad of armed policemen, showing how scared of them Mira feels. It also suggests that Mira finds herself so out of place as to feel almost criminally guilty.

Version 2

Mira's posture:

What's going to happen next?

Mira gives the best performance of her life.

The curtain rose, and the audience gasped as one as they saw Mira standing in the spotlight as serene as a fairy queen........... With the clatter of a drum riff, the band came to life around her.

With this simile, we get the impression that Mira feels magical: capable of anything. To the audience she seems something more than human.

Version 3

Mira's posture:

What's going to happen next?

Mira stops the band and starts shouting insults at the audience.

The curtain rose, and the audience gasped as one as they saw Mira standing in the spotlight like a fighting bull. With the clatter of a drum riff, the band came to life around her.

If a fighting bull is standing, but not yet charging, we wonder what it might be about to do: what violent chaos it is poised to unleash.

EXERCISE 6: STEAM TRAIN

Re-write the following passage, adding two similes.

The locomotive burst from the tunnel in a bulging cloud of smoke and steam. Noah pushed himself against the bank as it tore past, battering him with surges of air. With one hand he held his cap to the top of his head, while with the other he clung to a root.

As the train disappeared, the sky became clear again. Noah puffed out his cheeks, straightened his shirt, and continued on his way.

....
....
....
....
....
....
....
....
....
....
....

Now have another go, adding **TOO MANY** similes. As you do so, think about how many is too many, and what the problem with them is.

....

....

....

....

....

....

....

....

....

....

....

....

....

....

....

EXERCISE 6: EXAMPLE ANSWERS

The locomotive burst from the tunnel like a rampaging dragon, in a bulging cloud of smoke and steam. Noah pushed himself against the bank as it tore past, battering him with surges of air. With one hand he held his cap to the top of his head, while with the other he clung to a root.

As the train disappeared, the sky became clear again. Noah puffed out his cheeks, straightened his shirt as meticulously as a courtier before a royal audience, and continued on his way.

There are lots of other places where you might have put your two similes. I've chosen to make the locomotive's sudden emergence as terrifying as possible, and to add some detail about Noah's personality, while not letting my similes be too near to one another.

Here's my version with too many similes:

The locomotive burst from the tunnel in a bulging cloud of smoke and steam, like a shot from a cannon. Like a frightened animal, Noah pushed himself against the bank as it tore past, battering him with surges of air. With one hand he held his cap to the top of his head, while with the other he clung to a root.

As the train disappeared, the sky became clear again, as quickly as the parting of clouds after a summer shower. Noah puffed out his cheeks, straightened his shirt, and continued on his way like a man late for work.

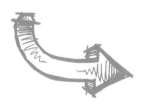

Taken together, the effect of these similes is overwhelming. The reader has to spend as much time imaging what things are like as thinking about how they are. It's hard to keep track of what's actually going on.

There's no rule to determine how many similes are too many. It's something you'll have to judge for yourself. However, if your first thought when inventing descriptions is always to reach for a simile, it's worth asking yourself whether you're neglecting other options.

FOLLOW-UP EXERCISE

Write a short description based on the following image. Aim to include some effective similes – but not too many!

....

....

....

....

....

....

....

....

....

....

....

....

....

....

....

....

Use this space if you'd like to try describing the scene in a different way:

....

....

....

....

....

....

....

....

....

....

....

....

....

blank page

PACK 8

Fantasy and Science Fiction Stories

WRITING A REALISTIC STORY ABOUT UNREALISTIC EVENTS

This pack will show you how to write convincingly about futuristic technology and magic!

FANTASY AND SCIENCE FICTION STORIES

This pack will show you how to write convincingly about futuristic technology and magic!

At the heart of all fiction writing is the suspension of disbelief.

Disbelief is the most normal state for a reader to be in. How often have you read a story while thinking something like this?

"These are just words on a page. These things didn't happen, and these characters aren't real."

After all, when you're reading a story, this is nothing but the truth!

But if you can't be persuaded to suspend your disbelief – to *imagine* that the events in the story are real – you won't care what happens. You'll put the book down and turn on the TV instead.

CHARACTER AND DISBELIEF

The surest way of all to lose a reader is to write characters who don't seem real.

> Two days later, Yuri's perception was blurred with mirages of tumbling water. He staggered onwards through the dust, pitching and staggering, still clutching the empty bottle in one hand. *Just one drop*, he thought. *Just one drop*.
>
> Rounding an abandoned outhouse, he came upon a fountain. He thought about his next holiday. It really was time for him to visit Europe – especially Paris. Yes, Paris it would be.

In the first paragraph of this example, Yuri seems very believable: a parched man, struggling through a dry land, dreaming of water.

Then he finds water, and seems neither surprised nor relieved. Instead, he thinks about doing a bit of tourism. This is described as though it's the most natural thing – not even the confusion of an exhausted person.

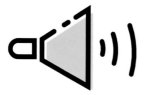 Because Yuri's thoughts and emotions don't seem real, he doesn't either. He's just a badly written character in a made-up scene.

However carefully you may paint your characters and bring them to life, what really counts is how they react to situations – especially when these situations are dramatic or stressful.

If they don't respond like real people, they won't seem real, and the reader won't care what else happens to them.

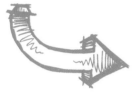

It may be that you're good at avoiding this sort of problem.

For one thing, it isn't too hard to make your characters believable when you write about things that you've experienced yourself.

When you wrote about a person stranded on a mountain, you could draw on your own memories of feeling scared and alone in a strange place: something that we've probably all experienced at some point in our lives. Those experiences will have given you a ready toolkit of thoughts and emotions to use in that story.

And of course, it's when you do this effectively that you really can suspend your reader's disbelief : your characters seem so perfectly real that your reader starts to believe that they aren't just reading about events, but are actually experiencing them.

But what happens when a plot goes crazy?

 How do make your characters believable when they go through things that you've never experienced?

 What about when things happen to them that *nobody* has ever experienced?

 As soon as you don't have relevant memories to draw on, writing realistic characters becomes a very special kind of challenge. This is one reason why your teachers may have warned you away from writing about gun battles and alien invasions!

THE VALUE OF FANTASY WRITING

Precisely because it's so difficult, crafting fantasy or science fiction stories with realistic characters is one of the most valuable exercises for a writer.

You've had so much practice by now that it's a challenge you're ready to take on!

In this pack, your task will be to write a story involving magic and some dramatic action. The challenge is to make your characters seem so real that all the things happening to them seem real too.

THINGS TO AVOID

Here are some things to beware of. Some of these apply particularly to fantasy and action stories; some are likely to be relevant to any piece of fiction!

BECOMING POWER-MAD

When you're writing about magic or futuristic technology, you can choose to make almost anything happen.

Just because you *can*, it doesn't follow that you *should*!

> Miles fought bravely as the ninjas closed in. He flicked spells to left and right, sending his adversaries catapulting away in Catherine wheels of gore. But it wasn't working. There were too many of them. Panting, he looked up, and the last thing he saw was the hatred on their faces as they flung the sack over his head and pinned him to the ground. He struggled in the darkness till his arms grew limp.
>
> This is it, he thought. The end.
>
> Clenching his fists weakly, he muttered the spell. "Ex", he panted. "Ca – Mo – Di" – one last desperate push – "Tor".
>
> With a flash and an ear-shuddering *whomp*, the room pulsed with energy and was silent.
>
> Miles wormed to his feet, shrugging the sack from his shoulders. Pieces of ninja lay messily against the walls. No sounds of footsteps came from the corridors beyond. "Time to go", he whispered to himself.

 You may not see anything obviously wrong with this. *But think about it!*

If Miles can save himself at any time by saying a magic word, why should we worry about anything else that happens to him? The next time that he's attacked, where will the tension be? Where's the drama, when we know that he can choose to kill his enemies at any moment?

What's more, why did he save his powers until he was pinned to the floor?

*Why did he think that it was **"the end"**, when he had a way to escape all along?*

If you create an imaginary world in which there are no rules, because there's always another secret spell or another fantastic piece of technology to be revealed on the next page – plucked from nowhere, like a rabbit from a conjurer's hat – you kill any chance for real tension and drama.

When you write about magic or futuristic technology, you give yourself unlimited, god-like power. However, if you want the reader to care about your characters, you also have to put limits on that power.

FLAT EMOTIONS

As we saw when discussing the example about Yuri in the desert, people's emotions need to be pitched at an appropriate level for the things they undergo. Powerful experiences produce intense emotional reactions.

ONE-SIDED EMOTIONS

Our feelings are complex and rarely one-dimensional.

 How often have you felt anger without also feeling a touch of shame, wounded pride, or excitement?

If your characters obviously feel only one thing at a time, they won't be wholly convincing.

LISTING THOUGHTS AND FEELINGS

Just because characters should have many emotions, it doesn't follow that you should be listing all of them!

 Try to show their feelings – through their appearance and their actions, for example – rather than telling the reader what they are.

Which of these options creates a more vivid emotional picture for you?

 As she saw it, she felt suddenly stressed. However, as she looked around, she realised that things were not so bad. Although she was confused, it occurred to her that the situation wasn't without humour.

 Her forehead jerked into a maze of tight creases; then she glanced to right and left with puzzled eyes, and her face relaxed. Her mouth twitched at one corner, with just a hint of a smile.

There's nothing wrong with saying what a character feels: sometimes it's the most economical approach.

However, whenever you can help your reader to work it out for themselves, try to do so.

 We go through our lives working out people's feelings from clues in their behaviour. People don't usually walk around with big signs saying "**I feel confused**" or "**My anger is intense but well hidden**". Try not to fix signs above their heads when you write about them!

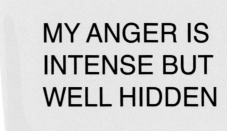

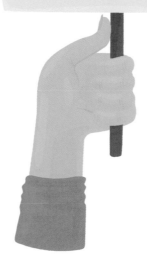

 The more involved a reader is in working out your characters for themselves, the less aware they will be that it's all just words on a page. Get their imagination working, and help them to create the story along with you.

TOO MUCH ACTION

It's easy to write a story that turns into a list of dramatic events:

Silvia dodged as the car screeched towards her. Twisting, she didn't manage to avoid the wing mirror, which sent her spinning across the road into the path of a lorry. Grabbing her broken ribs, she flung herself flat and let the vehicle pass over her, clearing her head by millimetres. Then she pulled the gun from her pocket and fired after the disappearing car. The rear windscreen exploded in a splash of glass, but the car kept on going. She radioed Gertrude, who swept down in the helicopter and threw her a rope. She hooked it to her belt and soared away to safety, cursing all the way.

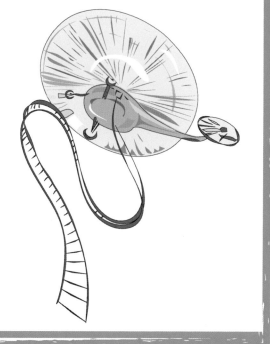

There's little here to make these extraordinary things seem real or emotionally important: nothing to help the reader imagine that they are really seeing them happen, let alone experiencing them.

In long stories, when a writer has already built convincing characters and gone some way to suspending the reader's disbelief, it is possible to fit in extended sections of frantic action. Without that groundwork in place, however, it doesn't work.

There are two options for solving the problem:

 Spread the action over considerably more space, taking enough time to make each event seem real and emotionally important: showing Silvia's emotions without their seeming one-sided, and describing the threats that she faces in a way that makes them genuinely alarming to the reader.

 For example, how did it feel to be struck by the car's wing mirror? How did Silvia know that her ribs were broken, and how did her feelings change as she made this discovery?

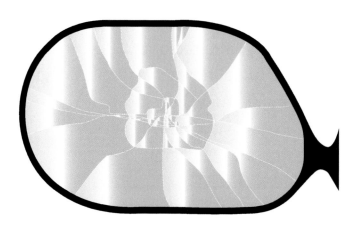

 Cut the plot back considerably, reducing the action to one or two key points that can be properly handled.

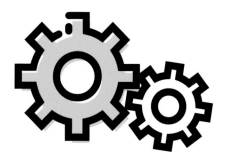

FOCUSING DESCRIPTION IN THE WRONG PLACES

Thandi stepped slowly across the logs, the ground soft beneath her feet. The smell of damp pine wood was thick about her, and she sighed as she thought once more of home. Then a monster attacked her, but she fought it off.

She sheathed her sword carefully, not wanting to risk its edge through clumsiness. She gulped and swallowed, then strode on into the settling dusk.

You could hardly accuse this writer of not being descriptive; yet the most important moment in this passage gets no description at all.

What matters more: the smell of the forest, or a desperate battle against an attacking monster?

The purpose of description is to make the story vivid and real for the reader. The more important or emotional an event is, the more descriptive effort you need to apply to it.

YOUR TASK

Write the first part of a story in which an elderly couple are kidnapped by aliens. The aliens have technology far more advanced than ours.

You should focus on the kidnapping itself. Your piece doesn't require a neat ending: there's no need to tie up the strands of your plot.

This task presents some serious challenges.

 As I've already discussed, this is a situation for which you are unlikely to have any relevant experience! How can you make the characters and their behaviour seem real?

 What's more, you have to write believably about people much older than you are – and about aliens!

 On the other hand, alien abduction is a remarkably conventional scenario, covered in any number of films and books. You need to find a way to be original and creative, and not write as though you're repeating ideas that you've picked up elsewhere.

 If these aliens have advanced technology, writing about it will be very like writing about magic. Making magic seem real involves working out its limits, and sticking to them.

 You need to avoid too much action. If your writing becomes a frantic list of events, it will seem empty: without emotion or meaningful characterisation.

PLANNING

Pack 3 (in Book 1) offered a lot of advice for planning. Now you're free to plan however you think best, using the space provided here. I suggest that you refer back to Pack 3 for ideas.

....

....

....

....

....

....

....

....

....

....

....

....

....

....

YOUR STORY

Now it's time for your first attempt.
You'll have the opportunity to try again later.

MY STORY

Here's my story. I'll explain what I've done afterwards, section by section.

The storm seemed to come from nowhere. One tight dark cloud, rushing in across a clear evening sky; a series of brisk flashes, and the sharp-fronted grumble of thunder; and then the rain. So much rain. An endless chute of water, like the outflow of an enormous tank: spattering from cars and roofs, sweeping away soil and gnomes from front gardens, launching it all whooshing down towards the centre of town.

Mr Deauville clutched his wife, as much for his own balance as for hers, his other arm reaching round to hold the sagging umbrella firm over their heads. "Oh dear, Boris," she called, struggling to make herself audible above the battering deluge. "It's pneumonia for you again." He squeezed her elbow and they resumed their shuffling struggle upstream. He had thought that his eye-roll was well hidden; her sly grin suggested otherwise.

Another bright flash came from somewhere nearby, and seconds later the thunder barked again. They held each other more closely, hunched lower, and pushed on.

Then they were slammed together as the world turned hot and white.

In that instant, Mrs Deauville knew with calm certainty that this was the end. It was good to feel Boris's solid form pressed against her. Her life did not pass before her eyes. She felt no fear or regret, nor even sublime relief. It simply – was. Time.

7385233 tilted forwards and extended a frond into the vanishing light, savouring its warmth. It sensed the life in the still figures curled on the deck below and felt the satisfaction of a mission well accomplished.

Still, the Earth aliens were so pointy and alarming, with their unretractable limbs and bony crania, and 7385233 perceived several disconcerting aromas. It had seen the holograms, but this reality was something else. The thought of sharing its ship with such unpleasant beings made its cilia quiver.

Still, only two more Satrektan months.

The male alien shifted and made a noise. He turned his head in bewilderment and obvious alarm, reaching for his female companion. She stirred and made noises of her own, and 7385233 saw the male's body relax slightly. "You were right, 4472645," the Trekt signalled in a rippling flourish of approval. "They are a bonded pair." It flicked out a frond in mock deference. "Perhaps you people do know how to unfold your brains after all." 4472645 bobbed ironically.

The sensation of gravity increased as the ship accelerated away from the planet. 7385233 felt its body compress uncomfortably. Weightlessness couldn't come soon enough.

It watched the aliens as they held each other close in their forelimbs. The female's eyes were making liquid. The male's were closed, his head pressed into his mate's mid-section.

4472645 rippled a signal. Its squad rolled gently, as unthreateningly as possible, towards their new guests. 7385233 watched through outstretched fronds. It almost believed that it could read these ugly creatures' emotions. Deep within it, something tightened with regret.

YOUR THOUGHTS

Just like in Pack 3, here's space for you to write your thoughts about my story and yours – before you read what I have to say about my choices.

What might we learn from each other's stories?

How could they be improved?

How well did we deal with the challenges listed on page 50?

....

....

....

....

....

....

....

....

....

....

....

....

....

MY STORY: SECTION BY SECTION

> The storm seemed to come from nowhere. One tight dark cloud, rushing in across a clear evening sky; a series of brisk flashes, and the sharp-fronted grumble of thunder; and then the rain. So much rain. An endless chute of water, like the outflow of an enormous tank: spattering from cars and roofs, sweeping away soil and gnomes from front gardens, launching it all whooshing down towards the centre of town.

 It isn't always a good idea in a short story to take time setting the scene. However, this opening serves twin purposes.

For one thing, it makes the location easy to relate to: this is a normal hillside town, with signs of comfortable ordinariness, such as parked cars, front gardens and plastic gnomes. Whatever happens in this story could happen anywhere.

On the other hand, the opening makes clear that something unusual is going on. A spectacular storm is caused by a single cloud in a clear sky – and there is so much water that the soil from gardens is washed away. This weather is freakish. Where has it come from, and what will happen next?

Careful vocabulary choices make the scene dramatic. The thunder "**grumbles**" – a slow, heavy sound – yet is "**sharp-fronted**", a way of conveying the *crack* at the start of a violent thunderclap when it is nearby: a sound to make you wince and cower. The rain is so fierce that it seems to fall in a "**chute**", more like a constant stream than a series of drops. A series of powerful verbs show its force when it hits the ground: "**spattering**", "**sweeping**" and "**whooshing**".

Mr Deauville clutched his wife, as much for his own balance as for hers, his other arm reaching round to hold the sagging umbrella firm over their heads. "Oh dear, Boris," she called, struggling to make herself audible above the battering deluge. "It's pneumonia for you again." He squeezed her elbow and they resumed their shuffling struggle upstream. He had thought that his eye-roll was well hidden; her sly grin suggested otherwise.

Another bright flash came from somewhere nearby, and seconds later the thunder barked again. They held each other more closely, hunched lower, and pushed on.

This section brings two characters into the story and helps us to understand and like them. We can tell that they are fairly old and perhaps less mobile than they once were. We also see humour in the way that they quietly and good-naturedly make fun of each other. This suggests a certain strength of character, bearing in mind the situation they find themselves in.

We get hints of how their personalities are different. Although Mr Deauville appears to support his wife, he is slyly using her as a balancing aid; yet he is prepared to put himself in an awkward position to make sure that the umbrella covers her. Mrs Deauville gently winds her husband up by making comments about his health. She's perceptive enough to spot when he secretly pulls a face, and finds this amusing rather than offensive.

They have the sort of relationship that many people would like to have in their old age.

The main purpose of this section, other than to be effective in its own right, is to help the reader feel emotionally involved when these characters are kidnapped.

> Then they were slammed together as the world turned hot and white.
>
> In that instant, Mrs Deauville knew with calm certainty that this was the end. It was good to feel Boris's solid form pressed against her. Her life did not pass before her eyes. She felt no fear or regret, nor even sublime relief. It simply – was. Time.

The moment at which they are struck by this mysterious force is described simply, reinforcing how overwhelming the experience is, as well as how little the characters understand it. The couple are thrown together, and all they really sense is that they are "**hot**" and surrounded by dazzling light.

Mrs Deauville's reaction shows her feeling ready for death. She is surprised not to have any of the thoughts commonly imagined in books – such as looking back on your life and wondering what could have been different, or simply being terrified. She is calm, and glad to be with her husband at this moment.

The purpose of this paragraph, apart from building our appreciation of Mrs Deauville's character, is to make her experience of *not* dying more of a jolt for the reader, as well as for her.

If you feel that it's the appropriate moment for your life to end without regret, it may be an unpleasant experience to look up a few seconds later and find yourself still alive.

In this story, I aimed to pull off the unusual trick of making the reader feel *sorry* that a likeable character is still alive. It's for you to judge whether this worked!

7385233 tilted forwards and extended a frond into the vanishing light, savouring its warmth. It sensed the life in the still figures curled on the deck below and felt the satisfaction of a mission well accomplished.

Still, the Earth aliens were so pointy and alarming, with their unretractable limbs and bony crania, and 7385233 perceived several disconcerting aromas. It had seen the holograms, but this reality was something else. The thought of sharing its ship with such unpleasant beings made its cilia quiver.

Still, only two more Satrektan months.

My story misses out a detailed description of the Deauvilles' journey up to the spaceship. There are enough clues at the point when they are thrown together by a beam of light – the same light that is fading away at the start of this new section.

More than this would risk seeming over the top and even silly, and it would be hard to avoid science fiction **clichés** (conventional, over-used ideas) while writing about tractor beams or teleportation. It's sometimes best to leave things to the reader's imagination!

As the first Trekt is introduced, we are made aware of its strangeness:

It has "**fronds**" rather than arms, and these fronds seem to sense things more vividly than our arms can. It is very aware of its "**cilia**" – little hairs.

From the fact that human "**unretractable**" limbs seem strange to this creature, it's a fair guess that a Trekt can draw its fronds back into its body. It also refers to humans' "**bony**" heads, so either its own head is soft, or it doesn't have one.

It "**tilts forwards**", which implies a rolling motion and thus a different body shape to ours.

 Perhaps most obviously, this alien has a number for a name.

On the other hand, there are several ways in which the Trekt may not seem so unfamiliar:

 It experiences emotions – even thoughts – such as we might: "**satisfaction**", curiosity, and even slight disgust when faced with an unfamiliar life-form. It's able to look at the coming two "**Satrektan months**", however long that might be, with a resigned mental shrug.

 It has a powerful sensory awareness, placing an emphasis on smell ("**aromas**") and touch ("**savouring its warmth**"). Although it probably exceeds our abilities, to the point of sensing "**life**", this alien seems to experience the universe in ways not wholly unfamiliar to us.

 Some of the concepts it thinks about – the "**deck**", images in the form of "**holograms**" – imply technological awareness and a way of ordering things that we might recognise.

Notice how much information is offered in hints, so that the reader has to work things out. This way, the reader is offered the chance to 'build a Trekt' in their own imagination; yet with so many clues, the Trekt in their head shouldn't be *too* different from the one in mine.

 It's often interesting to explore how your writing can present ideas and characters from different perspectives, and this section is a good example of that. The story is still about Mr and Mrs Deauville – but now, seen from the Trekt's perspective, they are strange, ugly, smelly aliens.

The male alien shifted and made a noise. He turned his head in bewilderment and obvious alarm, reaching for his female companion. She stirred and made noises of her own, and 7385233 saw the male's body relax slightly. "You were right, 4472645," the Trekt signalled in a rippling flourish of approval. "They are a bonded pair." It flicked out a frond in mock deference. "Perhaps you people do know how to unfold your brains after all." 4472645 bobbed ironically.

The sensation of gravity increased as the ship accelerated away from the planet. 7385233 felt its body compress uncomfortably. Weightlessness couldn't come soon enough.

It watched the aliens as they held each other close in their forelimbs. The female's eyes were making liquid. The male's were closed, his head pressed into his mate's mid-section.

There are many more clues about Trekts in this section. This time I won't list them!

Instead, here's some space for you to draw a Trekt as you imagine it, based on all the available information:

This section develops two main themes in parallel:

 We follow the emotions of the elderly couple as they awaken. These emotions are alien to the Trekts but obvious to us. We can recognise that Mr Deauville is worried that his wife might be dead, and feels relieved when she moves and makes a noise. From 7385233's perspective, Mrs Deauville's eyes "**make liquid**"; but *we* know that she is crying.

 We follow the exchange between the Trekts, who seem to view the humans as objects to be studied: apparently as some sort of scientific project. The repartee between 7385233 and 4472645, marked by exaggerated gestures ("**rippling flourish**") and irony, suggests a relationship in which 7385233 has more power, but respects its colleague.

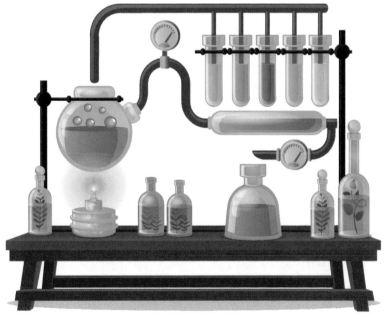

 These plot strands strengthen our sympathy for the kidnapped couple, while also helping us relate to the aliens. After all, the Trekts seem good-humoured, and they only want to study the Deauvilles in the same way that a human scientist might want to study a pair of unfamiliar animals. Is it fair to see these aliens as 'baddies'?

4472645 rippled a signal. Its squad rolled gently, as unthreateningly as possible, towards their new guests. 7385233 watched through outstretched fronds. It almost believed that it could read these ugly creatures' emotions. Deep within it, something tightened with regret.

 In stories where humans encounter alien species, a common theme sees people amazed to realise that the 'space animals' they've encountered in fact have sophisticated thoughts and emotions.

Here, this story turns that convention on its head: an alien is disturbed by the possibility that the humans it has kidnapped might experience the world like it does.

The story ends with 7385233 feeling "**regret**". We are left to wonder whether it will have the courage to do something about this feeling.

You can make a creature seem alien just through an unusual choice of verb. "**Rippled**" would be a mystifying choice to describe a human gesture, so it effectively emphasises how strange these aliens are – at the same time that the story explores how similar their personalities might be to our own.

TIME FOR ANOTHER GO

After all this, you probably have many ideas for improving or completely rewriting your story.

You can use this answer space to do so.

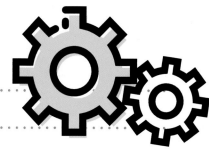

···

···

···

···

···

···

···

···

···

···

···

···

···

···

···

···

···

···

···

···

···

···

FOLLOW-UP TASK

If you'd like some more practice, have a go at the following task.

Write the first chapter of a story in which you discover that your best friend has magical abilities.

PACK 9

Verbs

HOW TO CHOOSE & USE THEM

Verbs are often overlooked, but they are one of your most powerful tools. This pack will help you to make them count.

VERBS

Verbs are often overlooked, but they are one of your most powerful tools. This pack will help you to make them count.

We'll start with a whirlwind tour of the ways that you'll most often encounter verbs, before we look at how to use them creatively in your writing.

A WHIRLWIND TOUR

This short guide offers a quick tour of what verbs are, as well as explaining some useful grammatical points. *You don't need to memorise everything!*

Yes, grammar can be boring – but the more you know about the building blocks of English, the better equipped you'll be to write effectively.

To help the most important ideas sink in, there are some simple exercises along the way.

Answers follow straight after each exercise.
When they're on the same page, I recommend covering the answers with a sheet of paper until you're ready to look at them.

You'll find it useful to refer back to this guide as you work on other RSL Creative Writing resources.

 If you want to skip to the section on using verbs effectively, it starts on page 109.

WHAT IS A VERB?

In simple terms, a verb is a word that indicates an action, a state of being or an occurrence.

- **An action:** The monkey climbs the wall.

- **A state of being:** The monkey was hairy.

- **An occurrence:** The drink becomes cloudy.

EXERCISE 1: SPOT THE VERBS

Underline the verbs in each sentence.

1 You are working hard today.

2 It is time to go to the shop.

3 The bird is singing.

4 Once upon a time, the princess lived in the tall tower.

5 It's time to get down to business.

EXERCISE 1: ANSWERS

1 You are working hard today.

2 It is time to go to the shop.

3 The bird is singing.

4 Once upon a time, the princess lived in the tall tower.

5 It's time to get down to business.

 "**'s**" is a verb, because "**it's**" is short for "**it is**".

"**Get down**" is a phrasal verb, which will be explained later on.

EXERCISE 2: ADD A VERB

Re-write each of these sentences with an additional verb, so that it makes sense. There will be many possible answers!

1 Yesterday the footballer his first goal.

....

2 Who will the cat while you're away?

....

3 That be the case, but in fact it isn't.

....

4 I wonder whether you really that.

....

5 How long will lunch to cook?

....

EXERCISE 2: EXAMPLE ANSWERS

 1 Yesterday the footballer scored his first goal.

>  Other possibilities include "**achieved**".

 2 Who will look after the cat while you're away?

> "**Feed**" would be another option.

 3 That should be the case, but in fact it isn't.

> "**May**", "**might**" or "**could**" wouldn't work, because we are told that whatever *should* be the case definitely *is not*. "**Should**" is a modal verb – which will be explained later on.

 4 I wonder whether you really believe that.

> There are lots of possibilities here! "**Like**" and "**think**" are examples.

 5 How long will lunch take to cook?

THE THREE BASIC VERB FORMS
Verbs have three basic forms.

You'll be most familiar with the base form:

 As an infinitive:
I like to eat cookies.

 In the present simple tense:
I write my essay before dinner
– or with an "**s**", Stephanie writes a story.

You are probably also comfortable with the past form, which is used for the past simple tense:

 I went to school.

 I lit the fire.

Finally, there's the "-ed" form (which unfortunately doesn't always end in "**-ed**"!), often used after the auxiliary verbs "**have**" and "**be**":

 I have closed the door.

 The crate was lifted onto the truck.

 With other endings:
It was given to my mum.
I have sung too many songs.

THE "-ING" VERB FORM: PRESENT PARTICIPLES AND GERUNDS

Apart from the three basic forms, you should be aware of the "-ing" form, which can indicate a present participle or a gerund.

A present participle describes an ongoing action – confusingly, not always in the present!

 In the present: Mahalia is walking back home.

 In the past: They were racing round the park.

A gerund is, essentially, a verb that ends in "**-ing**" and pretends to be a noun:

 The cleaning took hours.

 Hector used to like racing.

A good way to check for a gerund is to see whether a conventional noun could be swapped into the same place:

 The work took hours.

 Hector used to like Harry.

TRANSITIVE AND INTRANSITIVE VERBS

Verbs can be split into two main groups, depending on whether or not they act on something.

Which of these sentences make sense?

○ I really need.

○ I really need coffee.

○ Tom will have.

○ Tom will have news.

 "Have" and **"need"** are verbs that need objects: things to act on.
The thing that they act on is a noun or a noun phrase.
They can only be transitive verbs.

What about these sentences?

○ You arrive school.

○ You arrive.

○ You arrive at school.

○ You arrive tomorrow.

 "Arrive" cannot be followed by a noun such as **"school"**.
It can stand by itself (**"you arrive"**) – or it needs a linking preposition (**"at"**) or an adverb (**"tomorrow"**).
It can only be an intransitive verb.

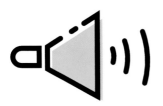

Don't be tricked when verbs are followed by something that is not a noun phrase. For example, consider this sentence:

The bird swept upwards.

The bird is not sweeping *something* upwards. "**Swept**" is an intransitive verb in this sentence, even though it is followed by the word "**upwards**". "**Upwards**" is an adverb, not a noun.

Many verbs can be used transitively or intransitively.

 I eat.

 I eat apples.

 Please sing!

 Please sing songs!

In order to write well, you need to be aware – at least instinctively – of whether you are using a transitive or an intransitive verb.

EXERCISE 3

In the following passage, circle each verb that is being used (transitively) and draw a box around each verb that is being used [intransitively].

Yesterday I grilled some burgers on the barbecue. Just as I was bending down with my plate, a splatter of fat dripped onto the charcoal. With a great whoosh, a tower of flame swept upwards and singed my hair. I leapt backwards with a yelp.

EXERCISE 3: ANSWERS

Yesterday I (grilled) some burgers on the barbecue. Just as I was [bending] down with my plate, a splatter of fat [dripped] onto the charcoal. With a great whoosh, a tower of flame [swept] skywards and (singed) my hair. I [leapt] backwards with a yelp.

This may well have been difficult, because *an intransitive verb can easily look transitive.* "**Dripped**", for example, is intransitive: the fat may drip "**onto the charcoal**" (notice the preposition, "**onto**"), but it doesn't "**drip the charcoal**".

CONDITIONAL SENTENCES

It's important that you know how to form conditional sentences correctly:

 If you ran quickly, you would arrive in time.

 You would arrive in time if you ran quickly.

 In both these cases, **"if you ran quickly"** is the conditional clause, while **"you would arrive in time"** is the main clause. As you can see from the examples, it's possible to play with the order of these clauses, depending on which idea you want to emphasise.

Here's a conditional sentence in the past:

 If you had been faster, you would have been in time.

 This sentence describes an event that has already been ruled out: there is now no possibility that you will be in time!

You'll have noticed that conditional sentences often require the use of **"would"**. **"Could"** is another possibility.

To describe something that is 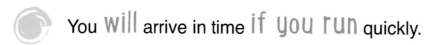 more likely to happen, you can also use "**will**":

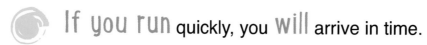 If you run quickly, you will arrive in time.

You will arrive in time if you run quickly.

Conditional sentences can use the subjunctive mood to show that a thing is *possible*, but not a fact. This is common in traditional or formal English:

If you were to run quickly, you'd arrive in time.

There are lots of other subjunctive constructions in English … but this is only a whirlwind tour!

EXERCISE 4

Rewrite the following conditional sentences, using "would" or "could" instead of "will" or "can".

1 Aditya will do well if she studies hard.

....

2 If you eat any more cookies, you'll become fat.

....

3 I'll be a lot happier if I can get all this washing-up done.

....

EXERCISE 4: ANSWERS

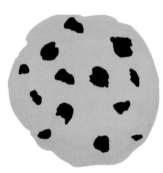

1 Aditya will do well if she studies hard.

Aditya would do well if she studied hard.

2 If you eat any more cookies, you'll become fat.

If you ate any more cookies, you'd become fat.

3 I'll be a lot happier if I can get all this washing-up done.

I'd be a lot happier if I could get all this washing-up done.

EXERCISE 5

Now do the same thing, the other way round!

1 I would be disappointed if you couldn't do it.

....

2 If they weren't sure, they would not risk it.

....

3 Derek would be a lot more confident if he could pass the exam.

....

EXERCISE 5: ANSWERS

1 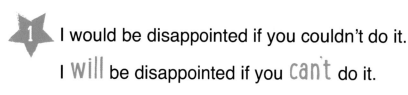 I would be disappointed if you couldn't do it.

I will be disappointed if you can't do it.

2 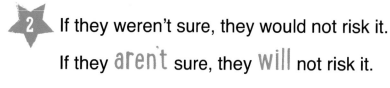 If they weren't sure, they would not risk it.

If they aren't sure, they will not risk it.

3 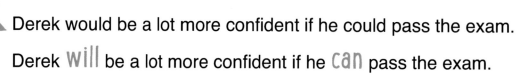 Derek would be a lot more confident if he could pass the exam.

Derek will be a lot more confident if he can pass the exam.

EXERCISE 6

Now take the same sentences using "would", and rewrite them with "would have" – to describe something that is no longer possible.

1 I would be disappointed if you couldn't do it.

....

2 If they weren't sure, they would not risk it.

....

3 Derek would be a lot more confident if he could pass the exam.

....

EXERCISE 6: ANSWERS

1 I would be disappointed if you couldn't do it.

I would have been disappointed if you couldn't have done it.

2 If they weren't sure, they would not risk it.

If they hadn't been sure, they would not have risked it.

3 Derek would be a lot more confident if he could pass the exam.

Derek would have been a lot more confident if he could have passed the exam.

EXERCISE 7

Rewrite each of the following sentences using the subjunctive mood.

1 If you'd help me, I'd get this done more quickly.

....

2 If you would only wait, I'd be with you soon!

....

3 Sonya would be a lot happier if her ice cream stopped melting.

....

EXERCISE 7: ANSWERS

1 If you'd help me, I'd get this done more quickly.

   If you were to help me, I'd get this done more quickly.

2 If you would only wait, I'd be with you soon!

   If you were only to wait, I'd be with you soon!

3 Sonya would be a lot happier if her ice cream stopped melting.

   Sonya would be a lot happier if her ice cream were to stop melting.

THE PAST PERFECT TENSE

Most people write confidently about events occurring at a single point in the past:

 I was walking to my friend's house when I saw the seagull.

However, it's easy to get in a tangle when you have to talk about things happening at different times in the past.

Here's an example of a common mistake:

 I was walking to the house where I was brought up.

Did they walk to the house, knock on the door, then go inside to be brought up?

The writer almost certainly intended this meaning:

 I was walking to the house where I had been brought up.

Now it's clear that they were returning to their childhood home for a visit.

The timeline looks like this:

Further in the past (use "had"): They were brought up.	**The past:** They walked to the house.	**Now:** They are telling me about their walk.

Whenever you are writing about the past and need to indicate an event even further in the past, you will need to use the past perfect tense – what you might think of as the "had" tense.

Here are some more examples:

- I was avoiding my homework. I hadn't been working for hours.

- I looked everywhere. Where had he got to?

- I was eating the dinner that I'd cooked for myself.

- I couldn't give the presentation because I had had no time to prepare.

 "Had had" may look wrong, but in this context it makes perfect sense.

EXERCISE 8: JAMES AND JOHN

This is a famous grammar puzzle, not invented by me!

Two students, James and John, had to describe a man who had suffered from (had) a cold in the past. Their teacher assessed their work.

 Add punctuation to the following sentence so that it makes sense in correct English:

James while John had had had had had had had had had had a better effect on the teacher.

EXERCISE 8: ANSWER

All of the following possibilities are correct:

James, while John had had "**had**", had had "**had had**"; "**had had**" had had a better effect on the teacher.

James, while John had had "**had had**", had had "**had**"; "**had had**" had had a better effect on the teacher.

James, while John had had "**had**", had had "**had had**". "**Had had**" had had a better effect on the teacher.

James, while John had had "**had had**", had had "**had**". "**Had had**" had had a better effect on the teacher.

THE FUTURE TENSE?

I should mention the future tense.

I often talk about it …
but according to some
grammar experts,
it doesn't exist!

English verbs usually change to show events in the past: "I sort **the letters**" becomes "I sorted **the letters**".

In many other languages, there is also a special verb form to talk about things in the future. In English, however, we need to use workarounds.

 In English we have to say something like *Barbara will go to work*, using the same base form, "**go**", that we use when talking about present events.

 An Italian would just say *Barbara andrà a lavoro*, where "**andrà**" means "**will go**": the "**-rà**" verb ending shows that the action will happen in the future.

In English, we tend to talk about the future using verbs in the present. Here are some other examples:

 I am running a race tomorrow.

 You are going to hate me.

Occasionally, we talk about the future from the point of view of the past:

 I was going to love the rollercoaster.

 He knew that he would regret his choice.

 Whether it's more accurate to talk about the "**future tense**" or the "**future** modality" in English, it's important to master the various ways in which you can describe events that haven't happened yet.

AUXILIARY AND MODAL VERBS

Auxiliary verbs **are used along with other verbs.**

Here are some examples:

 You *are* studying.

 I *have* finished.

A *modal verb* is a kind of auxiliary, usually showing how *likely* or *important* something is:

 You *should* take a break.

 You *might* choose to look at this.

There are ten modal verbs in English:

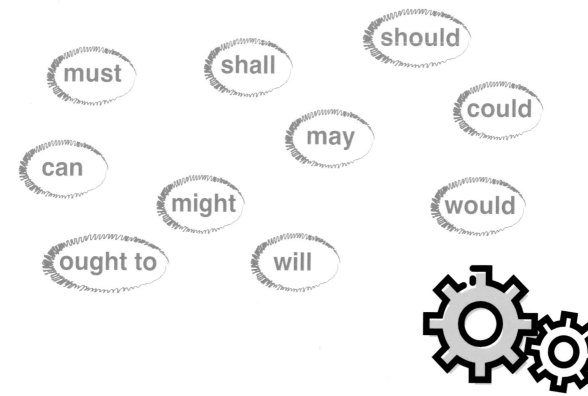

EXERCISE 9

In the following passage, (circle) each modal or auxiliary verb.

I am amazed by people's clumsiness almost every day. It really should be no surprise by now, but that's the way it is. I will get used to it at some point, I suppose, but I can't imagine it now. Might I ask whether you've broken a mug this week? I really will eat my hat if you deny it.

EXERCISE 9: ANSWERS

I (am) amazed by people's clumsiness almost every day. It really (should) be no surprise by now, but that's the way it is. I (will) adapt to it at some point, I suppose, but I (can)'t imagine it now. (Might) I ask whether you('ve) broken a mug this week? I really (will) eat my hat if you deny it.

 "**Can**" is a modal verb, but "**can't**" as a whole isn't: the word "**not**" isn't a verb at all.

 "**'ve**" is an auxiliary verb because it's short for "**have**" in the phrase "**you have broken**". The "**you**" part of "**you've**" is a pronoun, not a verb.

 If you're wondering why "**might**" in "**might I ask**" is a modal verb, bear in mind that if you took away the question, the word order would change to "**I might ask**" – with "**might**" directly modifying (changing) the verb.

PHRASAL VERBS

Compare these sentences:

 I need to catch the ball.

 I need to catch up with Clara.

 Edward will take the rucksack.

 Watch that plane take off!

 I will get a present at Christmas.

 I wonder whether I will get over the disappointment.

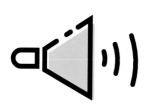

In each case, the combination of a verb and a particle creates a new meaning. For example, "**take off**" includes the verb "**take**", but means something entirely different.

This is known as a phrasal verb: a phrase that acts as a verb.

English is full of verbs like this. See how many you can spot as you read and write!

REFLEXIVE VERBS

There may be somebody who teaches you creative writing.

However, the fact that you are using these resources shows that you are also teaching yourself creative writing.

 "Teaching yourself" is an example of a reflexive verb construction.

 "Yourself", meanwhile, is a reflexive pronoun.

A reflexive verb phrase uses a transitive verb: a verb that describes one thing acting on another. Where the subject and object of a transitive verb are *different*, you have a sentence like this:

 I asked you what was going on.

↑   ↑

Subject **Object**

When the subject is *the same* as the object – in other words, it does something to *itself* – you end up with a sentence like this:

 I asked **myself** what was going on.

↑ **Subject**   ↑ **Reflexive pronoun**

Here are the main reflexive pronouns:

 I feed **myself** cookies.

 You take **yourself** very seriously.

 He introduced **himself** to the delegation.

 She took **herself** elsewhere.

 The battery exhausted **itself** in minutes.

 We allowed **ourselves** to relax.

 You really set **yourselves** up for that!

 They washed **themselves** before swimming.

When you want to talk about somebody without specifying whether they are male or female, you might use the reflexive pronoun "**themselves**" to talk about a single person:

 That person really loves themselves.

Occasionally, this is written as "**themself**" – although many people would regard this as incorrect:

 That person really loves themself.

"**Themself**" is best avoided, except in very informal writing. I don't much like it myself!

Just occasionally, you might also see this reflexive pronoun:

 It's important to look after oneself.

The use of "one" and "oneself" used to be very widespread in English, especially when talking about an idea without reference to a specific person: when talking about people in general. Nowadays it's a little less common.

ACTIVE AND PASSIVE VERBS

You'll have used active and passive verbs countless times. Nevertheless, you're likely to use them a lot better once you know what they are.

A verb is active when the verb's subject is *performing* an action:

A verb is passive when the verb's subject *undergoes* an action.

You'll usually choose between active and passive constructions based on the meaning you want to convey.

 If you're a Spanish sports journalist, you'll probably write that "**Real Madrid** beat **Manchester United**".

 If you're from Manchester, you'll be more inclined to focus on your own team's failure and write that "**Manchester United** were beaten by **Real Madrid**".

In some situations a passive construction shows that we know who the victim of an action is, but not who did it:

 The man has been mugged.

If you're interrupted doing something naughty, perhaps a passive construction will come naturally:

"**What's going on here?**"

"**The window got broken.**"

(Of course, "**got**" isn't quite right here. "**Has been**" would be correct.)

How many times have you said something like this, to avoid an admission such as "I broke the window"?

Passive constructions often look awkward. **"The phone is being played with by Mahalia"** is ugly: you should almost certainly write **"Mahalia is playing with her phone"**.

When you could pick either, it's usually best to go for an active construction. Save passive verbs for when you really need them.

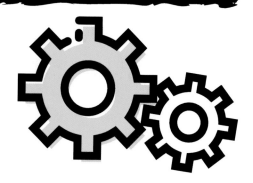

EXERCISE 10

Rewrite each of these sentences to make the verb construction active.

1 The tea is sold by Tesco.

....

2 The structure of a sentence is determined by its intended meaning.

....

3 The violin is being played by the maestro.

....

EXERCISE 10: ANSWERS

 The tea is sold by Tesco.

Tesco sells the tea.

 The structure of a sentence is determined by its intended meaning.

The intended meaning of a sentence determines its structure.

 The violin is being played by the maestro.

The maestro is playing the violin.

EXERCISE 11

Rewrite each of these sentences using a passive verb.

1 Hans chewed the toy.

....

2 The wind batters the canopy.

....

3 The ingredients of an apple pie influence its taste.

....

EXERCISE 11: ANSWERS

 1 Hans chewed the toy.

The toy was chewed by Hans.

 2 The wind batters the canopy.

The canopy is battered by the wind.

 3 The ingredients of an apple pie influence its taste.

The taste of an apple pie is influenced by its ingredients.

THE END OF THE TOUR!

It may be that much of the information in this guide won't directly change how you write. However, it *should* (a modal verb!) still be very useful.

Before you know any grammar, English can seem like a mess of choices.

> I could do this or that, while this other thing sounds wrong – but why?

As soon as you can put names to things, however, language becomes more of a toolbox of options:

> I've written "**should**", which is a modal verb. Would another modal verb, such as "**might**" or "**may**", be more appropriate?

When a sentence sounds wrong, or somebody else *points out* (a phrasal verb) a mistake in your work, you'll have a much better chance than before of understanding what went wrong.

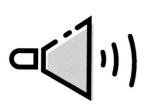 Lastly, you'll be in a position to understand the things that I say when I write about verbs in these creative writing resources!

Refer back to this guide whenever you have the opportunity.

 Now that we've covered the main kinds of verb, let's think about how to use them most effectively.

VAGUE AND SPECIFIC VERBS
Compare these two paragraphs:

1

Alice ran across the playground. The tile was on the edge of the roof, about to fall onto the children standing below. "Run, Thomas! Katie!" she shouted.

2

Alice flung herself across the playground. The tile was quivering on the edge of the roof, about to plummet onto the children huddled below. "Run, Thomas! Katie!" she screamed.

There is nothing incorrect about the first paragraph, but the second one is far more vivid.

The verbs in the second paragraph are more interesting. However, what really counts is that they are more specific.

Many of the verbs in the first passage raise questions:

 How did she run? Was she moving confidently, or in a panic?

 Was the tile still or moving? If it was just resting there, why did Alice think that it would fall?

 How were the children standing? Were they just loitering, or were they doing something?

 What emotion did Katie show when she shouted?

The second passage includes verbs that show **exactly what is happening**.

What's more, every verb carries strong emotion:

When we read that Alice "**flung herself**" (a reflexive verb) towards her friends, we know how much of a panic she was in – without needing to be told.

When we learn that the tile was "**quivering**", we can visualise it wobbling on the edge, just about to fall: we understand exactly why Alice was so desperate to warn her friends.

"**Huddled**" helps us to imagine Alice's friends crouched together – a compact, easy target for the falling tile – and suggests that something important was distracting them from the danger.

 Effective verbs may be a more powerful descriptive tool than anything else you will study in this course.

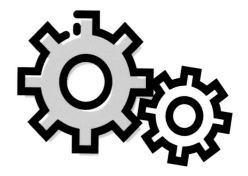

EXERCISE 12: DAYSTAR

Here's a passage with some rather vague verbs, highlighted below.

The lightning came down in a jagged fork, burning the tree beside the stables. A few seconds passed. Then, with a tremendous crash, thunder sounded against the roof. Daystar turned his head, his eyes opening, then stood up on his hind legs – and bolted. He pushed through the doors and ran away down the track, his hooves landing on the earth.

Now fill in the gaps, replacing the vague and ineffective verbs with specific, more effective choices.

The lightning . . . . down in a jagged fork, ... the tree beside the stables. A few seconds passed. Then, with a tremendous crash, thunder . . . . through the roof. Daystar . . . . his head, his eyes opening, then . . . . up on his hind legs – and bolted. He . . . . through the doors and . . . . away down the track, his hooves . . . . the earth.

EXERCISE 12: EXAMPLE ANSWER

The lightning plunged down in a jagged fork, torching the tree beside the stables. A few seconds passed. Then, with a tremendous crash, thunder hammered against the roof. Daystar jerked his head, his eyes opening, then reared up on his hind legs – and bolted. He crashed through the doors and charged away down the track, his hooves pounding the earth.

EXERCISE 13: THE CRASH

Fill in the gaps with effective verbs. Pay attention to word endings when these are provided.

The plane was ....ing low across the glacier when the storm cloud ....ed in from behind the mountain. The first thing the pilot knew about it was when her craft ....ed right, and then further right, for all that she .... to .... back the stick. The world ....ed in the dirty whiteness of spoiled milk. The wind ....ed, ...ing through the cabin. Then the plane ....ed back into daylight – just in time for the pilot to see the rock face ....ing towards her.

EXERCISE 13: EXAMPLE ANSWER

The plane was sweeping low across the glacier when the storm cloud flooded in from behind the mountain. The first thing the pilot knew about it was when her craft veered right, and then further right, for all that she fought to haul back the stick. The world vanished in the dirty whiteness of spoiled milk. The wind wailed, battering through the cabin. Then the plane snapped back into daylight – just in time for the pilot to see the rock face rushing towards her.

WHEN ADVERBS TAKE OVER

The next paragraph shows what usually happens when somebody understands the importance of creating strong emotions, but doesn't know how to use verbs effectively.

> Alice ran frantically across the playground. The tile was on the edge of the roof, about to fall lethally onto the children standing complacently below. "Run, Thomas! Katie!" she shouted in desperation.

This conveys most of the same information as the improved text above, but in a clumsy way.

- The verb-adverb phrases "**ran frantically**", "**fall lethally**" and "**standing complacently**" are very repetitive.

- "**Shouted in desperation**" avoids this problem – it's better than "**shouted desperately**", with yet another adverb, would have been – but it's still wordy.

Let's have another look at my improved version:

Alice flung herself across the playground. The tile was quivering on the edge of the roof, about to plummet onto the children huddled below. "Run, Thomas! Katie!" she screamed.

This is much more effective than the version with lots of adverbs. It's cleaner and easier to read, as well as more dramatic.

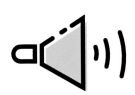

Adverbs can be effective when used well.

However, whenever you find yourself reaching for an adverb to spice up a verb, ask yourself whether a more precise verb would do the same job better.

EXERCISE 14

In each of the following sentences, replace the verb and adverb with a single verb (which could be a phrasal verb) that conveys a similar idea.

1 The explosion sounded loudly through the city.

The explosion .... through the city.

2 Ronald is eating his dinner quickly.

Ronald is .... his dinner.

3 Did you see how Preeti jumped athletically over the bar?

Did you see how Preeti .... over the bar?

4 The binman paused, thoughtfully watching the sunrise.

The binman paused, ... the sunrise.

5 The wet pavement shines brightly in the moonlight.

The wet pavement .... in the moonlight.

EXERCISE 14: EXAMPLE ANSWERS

There are many alternative possibilities! It's unlikely that your answers will match mine, but they should convey the same broad ideas.

1 The explosion boomed through the city.

2 Ronald is gulping down his dinner.

3 Did you see how Preeti sprang over the bar?

4 The binman paused, contemplating the sunrise.

5 The wet pavement gleams in the moonlight.

EXERCISE 15: TOM AND THE ROBIN

This passage is full of dull verbs and unnecessary verb-adverb combinations. Replace all of them!

The robin moved across the lawn, leaving patches of rapidly moving grass in its wake. Tom sat, his hind quarters moving to and fro, his eyes narrow. Suddenly, where seconds before there had been a jolly little bird, there was a noisily growling whirlwind of claws and quickly moving fur. Then Tom stopped suddenly. He moved a paw unbelievingly through empty space. Above him, a little bird sat on a telephone line and twittered.

The robin .... across the lawn, leaving patches of .... grass in its wake. Tom .... his hind quarters .... , his eyes narrow. Suddenly, where seconds before there had been a jolly little bird, there was a .... whirlwind of claws and .... fur. Then Tom .... He .... a paw unbelievingly through empty space. Above him, a little bird .... on a telephone line and twittered.

EXERCISE 15: EXAMPLE ANSWER

The robin skipped across the lawn, leaving patches of quivering grass in its wake. Tom crouched, his hind quarters wriggling, his eyes narrow. Suddenly, where seconds before there had been a jolly little bird, there was a snarling whirlwind of claws and flailing fur. Then Tom stiffened. He swished a paw unbelievingly through empty space. Above him, a little bird squatted on a telephone line and twittered.

EXERCISE 16: YEVGENIYA KUZNETSOVA

Rewrite this passage, changing whichever verbs and verb-adverb combinations you think can be improved. **If you think that something doesn't need to be changed, leave it as it is!**

Yevgeniya Kuznetsova sat back slowly into the chair, moving a pen agitatedly between the fingers of her left hand while her right forefinger stroked the stem of a martini glass. The intercom on her desk squealed. She put her palm onto the cut-off and the pen travelled rapidly away, landing noisily against the wall's oak panels. That was better, she thought. Silence. She crossed her white-socked feet on the desk blotter and looked out of her four-hundredth floor window, watching the clouds move past just below. She closed her eyes and sighed.

EXERCISE 16: EXAMPLE ANSWER

I've highlighted all my changes in the answer below.

Yevgeniya Kuznetsova settled back into the chair, twiddling a pen between the fingers of her left hand while her right forefinger stroked the stem of a martini glass. The intercom on her desk squealed. She slammed her palm onto the cut-off and the pen skewed away, clattering against the wall's oak panels. That was better, she thought. Silence. She crossed her white-socked feet on the desk blotter and gazed out of her four-hundredth floor window, watching the clouds scoot past just below. She closed her eyes and sighed.

 You might have made different choices. However, some things are important. For example, "**sat back slowly**" is a fairly clumsy phrase, for which there are many potential alternatives. On the other hand, verbs such as "**squealed**" and "**sighed**" are already doing a good job: there's no strong reason to mess with them.

EXERCISE 17: YOU VS ROBERT LOUIS STEVENSON

Now you've had the chance to practise your use of verbs, let's see how your work compares to a famous author's!

The following passage has been slightly adapted from *Treasure Island*, by Robert Louis Stevenson. I've changed a number of verbs to make them less effective. All the changed verbs are highlighted:

I opened my eyes at once. All round me were little ripples, combing over with a sharp, bristling sound and slightly phosphorescent. The Hispaniola herself, a few yards in whose wake I was still being moved along, seemed to move less easily in her course, and I saw her spars move a little against the blackness of the night. As I looked longer, I made sure she also was turning to the southward.

I looked over my shoulder, and my heart moved against my ribs. There, right behind me, was the glow of the camp-fire. The current had turned at right angles, moving round along with it the tall schooner and the little 3 coracle; ever quickening, ever moving higher, ever muttering louder, it went turning through the narrows for the open sea.

Suddenly the schooner in front of me gave a violent yaw, turning, perhaps, through twenty degrees; and almost at the same moment one shout followed another from on board. I could hear feet making noise on the companion ladder and I knew that the two drunkards had at last been interrupted in their quarrel and awakened to a sense of their disaster.

I opened my eyes at once. All round me were little ripples, combing over with a sharp, bristling sound and slightly phosphorescent. The Hispaniola herself, a few yards in whose wake I was still being .... along, seemed to .... in her course, and I saw her spars .... a little against the blackness of the night. As I looked longer, I made sure she also was .... to the southward.

I .... over my shoulder, and my heart .... against my ribs. There, right behind me, was the glow of the camp-fire. The current had turned at right angles, ... round along with it the tall schooner and the little .... coracle; ever quickening, ever .... higher, ever muttering louder, it went .... through the narrows for the open sea.

Suddenly the schooner in front of me gave a violent yaw, turning, perhaps, through twenty degrees; and almost at the same moment one shout followed another from on board. I could hear feet .... on the companion ladder and I knew that the two drunkards had at last been interrupted in their quarrel and awakened to a sense of their disaster.

EXERCISE 17: STEVENSON'S ANSWER

Here's the same passage, with the verbs *actually* used by Robert Louis Stevenson:

I opened my eyes at once. All round me were little ripples, combing over with a sharp, bristling sound and slightly phosphorescent. The Hispaniola herself, a few yards in whose wake I was still being whirled along, seemed to stagger in her course, and I saw her spars toss a little against the blackness of the night. As I looked longer, I made sure she also was wheeling to the southward.

I glanced over my shoulder, and my heart jumped against my ribs. There, right behind me, was the glow of the camp-fire. The current had turned at right angles, sweeping round along with it the tall schooner and the little dancing coracle; ever quickening, ever bubbling higher, ever muttering louder, it went spinning through the narrows for the open sea.

Suddenly the schooner in front of me gave a violent yaw, turning, perhaps, through twenty degrees; and almost at the same moment one shout followed another from on board. I could hear feet pounding on the companion ladder and I knew that the two drunkards had at last been interrupted in their quarrel and awakened to a sense of their disaster.

Your verbs will almost certainly have been different.

 Whose choices were more effective?

 Why do you think this?

 What can you learn from the differences between your choices and Stevenson's?

EXERCISE 18: FREE DESCRIPTION

Write brief descriptions of the following scenarios, using the space provided.
Above all else, focus on using verbs as effectively as possible!

➡️ An alien spaceship lands in a school playground.

....

....

....

....

....

....

....

....

➡️ A spider catches a fly in its web.

....

....

....

....

....

....

....

....

EXERCISE 18: EXAMPLE ANSWERS

Here's what I've done with the tasks given above. I've highlighted what I think are the most interesting verbs and verb constructions.

➡️ **An alien spaceship lands in a school playground.**

The pyramid lowered itself[1] towards earth with a tremendous grinding sound, like a million forks scraping on tin dishes[2]; yet the dry leaves barely shifted. The morning breeze played lightly[3] at their edges, as though the strange craft were not[4] roaring and tearing[5] a mere metre above them. Two hundred small faces stared in fearful fascination, standing as far back as their curiosity would bear[6], as still as the leaves themselves. The ship eased down with a heavy crunch, and the great scraping[7] sank back to a whir – and then to silence.

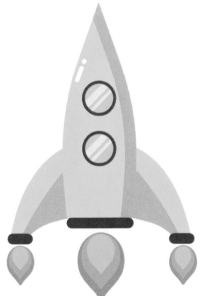

¹ A reflexive verb, using the reflexive pronoun **"itself"**

² A good simile is worth the effort, if it creates a clear impression in the reader's mind. In this case, you're encouraged to think of a rather high-pitched noise – not the deep roar of an aeroplane engine, for example – and of how it might make you cringe, like a fork scratching a metal plate.

³ Adverbs aren't always bad!

⁴ This is **subjunctive**, because I'm talking about a **hypothetical** – imaginary – situation in which the "**strange craft**" is *not* just above the leaves.

⁵ Notice how many verbs I've used to describe the sound of the spaceship: "**grinding**", "**scraping**", "**roaring**" and "**tearing**". Taken together, these give a much richer impression of its noise than any one verb might have done.

⁶ "**Bear**" implies that the children's curiosity is like a burden that they must sustain.

⁷ This is a **gerund**: a verb behaving as a noun (notice the use of "**the**" in "**the scraping**"). "**Scraping**" is repeated from the first sentence. Repetition is usually best avoided, but here it works as a reminder, emphasising the difference between the initial noise and this new quietness.

A spider catches a fly in its web.

It fizzed in like a missile and slammed[1] onto the webbing. The tough thread bowed like a trampoline before snapping back, and the whole web bucked and swayed[2]. The spider became rigid for a second, then set to work, testing – tasting[3] – the thread with its forelegs. Then it sprang, scurrying with unswerving certainty. Enveloping[4] the fly in its limbs, it immersed its mouthparts in the soft body. Soon the web was[5] still.

[1] These powerful, violent verbs might seem surprising when describing something as small as a fly. They help the reader to think about things from the perspective of a tiny creature, for whom flying at full speed into a web would not be a trivial matter.

[2] The four verbs in this sentence were carefully chosen to show exactly how the web moves after the impact. Think about how "**bucked**" and "**swayed**" describe different movements, and how they combine to create a vivid picture.

[3] The spider isn't literally "**tasting**" the thread. What effect does it create when a verb suggests the 'wrong' sense, as this one does?

[4] When somebody is "**enveloped**" in limbs, this might suggest a hug. The very different situation here makes this verb choice sinister.

[5] There's nothing wrong with a simple verb in the right place. After all the drama, the ordinariness of this sentence emphasises that everything is over – for the fly, at least.

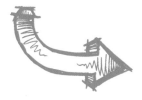

If these examples have given you some new ideas, why not have another go?

FOLLOW-UP EXERCISE

Write a short story about a private detective following somebody through a city at night. Focus on using verbs as effectively as you can.

....

....

....

....

....

....

....

....

....

....

....

....

....

....

Made in the USA
Middletown, DE
27 November 2021

53476188R00075